KNOWLEDGE ENCYCLOPEDIA
MAMMALS

© Wonder House Books 2024

All rights reserved. No part of this book may be reproduced or transmitted in any form by any means, electronic or mechanical, including photocopying and recording, or by any information storage and retrieval system except as may be expressly permitted in writing by the publisher.

Wonder House
(An imprint of Prakash Books)

contact@wonderhousebooks.com

Disclaimer: The information contained in this encyclopedia has been collated with inputs from subject experts. All information contained herein is true to the best of the Publisher's knowledge.

ISBN : 9789354402500

Table of Contents

The World of Mammals	3
What Makes a Mammal?	4–5
A Blast from the Past	6–7
Mammalian Orders	8–9
The Carnivore at the Top	10–11
The Killer Whale	12
The Intelligent Dolphins	13
Predators of the Night	14
The Prowling Tiger	15
The Agile Fox	16
The Galloping Horse	17
The Graceful Deer	18
The Unique Rodents	19
The Herbivorous Hippo	20
The Strong Elephant	21
All About Marsupials	22
The Playful Seal	23
The Intelligent Primates	24–25
Our Evolution	26–27
How Babies Are Born	28–29
From Here to There	30
Conservation of Endangered Mammals	31
Word Check	32

THE WORLD OF MAMMALS

Mammals have lived on Earth for a long time! They are classified as species that give birth to their young (not by laying eggs), and whose females feed their babies with milk from their bodies. So, even human beings are classified as mammals.

The earliest known mammals were the tiny morganucodontids that lived 210 million years ago alongside the mighty dinosaurs. When a huge asteroid or comet struck Earth, the dinosaurs were wiped out and the mammals had a chance to grow and evolve.

Today, many diverse species of animals roam the Earth. Small mammals like the thumb-sized pygmy shrew and large mammals like the blue whale are a mark of mammalian diversity as are tall giraffes and flying bats. Read on to find out more about this vast group of animals.

▶ Giraffes are the tallest mammals on our planet

What Makes a Mammal?

Mammals are classified as 'Mammalia'. This class of animals have a few unique features that make them the highest order of beings residing on the planet. Besides giving birth to their young and feeding them milk from their own bodies, there are other features that determine whether an animal species is a mammal.

Hair

Hair refers to small thread-like projections that emerge from the outermost layer of the mammal's skin. It is also called the fur or animal coat. All mammals possess this trait, though they may have hair in varied appearances and at different stages of their lives.

Dolphins have small pits at the snout, where they had hair at the time of their birth. Dolphin calves in their mother's womb have these pits filled with hair, but after birth, the hairs fall off while swimming. Animals like elephants and rhinoceroses have sparse, bristly hair, while polar bears have a long, thick fur to keep warm in the cold Arctic. Human beings are among the mammals that have lesser hair.

Warm Blood

Mammals are warm-blooded animals. In other words, unlike amphibians or fish, they can maintain their body temperature, regardless of being out in the snow or sunlight. Their average body temperature varies between 36.7° C and 37.2° C. This ability of mammals to produce heat within their own bodies is called **endothermy**.

How do mammals maintain their body temperature? They might shiver. This action increases the heat that their bodies produce. To keep cool, they might pant or sweat, which leads to heat loss. Some mammals might hibernate. This reduces the heat in the body as other bodily functions slow down.

▲ Naked mole rats cannot control their body temperatures very well, so they like to live in tunnels to keep cool

▲ Polar bears need their fur to keep warm in freezing habitats

▶ A lioness with her cub; according to experts, there are only about 20,000 of these fierce cats left in the wild

ANNIMALS MAMMALS

Giving Birth

Majority of mammals (with the exceptions of the duck-billed platypus and echidna) do not lay eggs. The mother bears the young ones inside her body in an organ called the uterus until birth. Such organisms are called **viviparous**. Except for **marsupials**, who carry the young ones in a pouch, mammals give birth to a well-developed baby. The time the **foetus** spends in the womb of the mother is called the gestation period, which differs in all animals. An elephant carries its baby for almost 22 months, while the Virginia opossum carries its baby for only 12–13 days.

Mammalian Milk

Once the baby is born, it is fed milk produced by a special organ called mammary glands. This unique characteristic defines mammals. Non-functional glands are seen in males too, but it is the females which carry glands that can produce milk to feed the baby.

In primitive animals like the duck-billed platypus, the glands express milk directly onto the skin or fur, which is then lapped up by the baby. Mammary glands are modifications of sweat glands, the organ that produces sweat.

◀ Bats have extraordinary hearing abilities

More Mammalian Features

In all other forms of **vertebrates**, the jaw is attached to the skull via a set of bones. However, in mammals, early on during evolution, the jaw hinged itself directly to the skull, to create a set of ear bones; this helps this class of organisms hear better. Also, mammals have different types of teeth, such as the molars, premolars, canines, and incisors. These specialised teeth help them grind and chew their food. The biggest evolutionary development in mammals is their big brain, which helps them think and reason better.

💡 Isn't It Amazing!

Humpback whales are very agile for their size. How does the huge animal manage to be so swift? That is because it has golf-ball sized bumps on its head and **pectoral fins**. They are **hair follicles** connected to sensitive nerves. Studies reveal it is these that help the whale in being swift. Also, the hair follicles are said to help the animal detect water currents and food.

▲ The Latin name for humpback whales is 'Megaptera novaeangliae', meaning 'big wing of New England'

👶 In Real Life

Elephants can overheat easily because they do not have a large skin surface in comparison to their body size. These animals do not sweat like human beings; instead, they use their skin to keep cool. If the skin heats up on a hot day or after a long walk, the internal heat generated cannot be reduced. This is where their hair comes to the rescue. It helps the body stay cool!

▲ Small, sharp hair seen on an elephant's head

A Blast from the Past

Though it might be hard to imagine, it took a long time for the different species of mammals to evolve into what we see today. If we want to read about the evolution of different mammals, we can do so because of the researchers and scientists who have unearthed fossils or remains of extinct mammals that existed long before the advent of human beings. Through the study of these fossils, scientists learned about the existence, behaviour, food habits, and extinction of ancient mammals.

Sabre-toothed Cats

If we were alive 42 million to 11,000 years ago, then we might have been able to spot sabre-toothed cats in the wild. Sadly, these mammals are extinct. They were said to live in North America and Europe as their fossils were found around these continents. There were different species of sabre-toothed cats and some of them prowled the wilds of South America too.

Sabre-toothed cats had short, bulky bodies and short tails when compared to modern lions. These vicious cats were known for their sabre-like teeth, which were very long and sharp. They were named after this feature.

▲ *It is misleading to call these animals sabre-toothed tigers as they are not closely related to modern tigers*

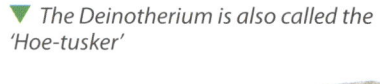

▼ *The Deinotherium is also called the 'Hoe-tusker'*

Deinotherium

The name *Deinotherium* means 'terrible beast'. At a glance, this large ancient mammal resembles the modern elephant. But compare them closely and their differences become clear. The *Deinotherium* had a shorter trunk and downward-facing tusks. Scientists believe they were used to pull down trees or dig out roots from underground. It was also much larger than the modern elephant, nearly 13 feet tall. It lived in Europe, Asia, and Africa. The African species outlasted the other two. The mammal disappeared around 7 million years ago.

Isn't It Amazing!

Even though they are named for their famous teeth, it is believed that at least two species of the sabre-toothed cats had weak jaws and bites. These mammals did not chase their prey. Instead, they ambushed it with their packs. They bit the prey but primarily used their neck muscles and forelimbs to hold it down and weaken it. Research has revealed that modern lions might have stronger bites than these ancient beasts!

ANIMALS | MAMMALS

🐾 Glyptodont

Think of the armadillo. Now, picture a creature that is much larger in size and weighs nearly 2,000 kilograms. It is the glyptodont. Compared to that, the modern armadillo (a distant cousin) only weighs up to 54 kilograms!

The glyptodont originated about 20 million years ago. It had a powerful spiky tail that was shaped like a club. It had a tough **carapace**—the bony outer shell covered with scales. It lived in South America and is said to have disappeared at the end of the last Ice Age, about 10,000 years ago.

▶ *The extinction of glyptodonts coincided with the arrival of early humans in the Americas*

🐾 Entelodont

The extinct entelodonts and modern pigs share a long, extended family. They might even have been related to the modern hippopotamuses. Fossil evidence shows that the entelodonts originated about 40 million years ago and became extinct 16–19 million years ago. These ancient mammals roamed in Asia, Europe, and North America.

The animals were medium or large with the heaviest species found to be nearly 900 kilograms. Naturally, they were much heavier than the modern pigs. The entelodonts probably had an **omnivorous** diet.

◀ *The entelodont had a fierce temper and was extremely fast*

👤 In Real Life

Along with the sabre-toothed cat, the woolly mammoths make the movie *Ice Age* interesting. In reality, they were as big as African elephants but had small ears, probably to keep out the cold of the Ice Age. They had very long tusks and were herbivores. They disappeared when the climate turned warmer.

▲ *As the name suggests, the woolly mammoth's body was covered with woolly hair to keep warm*

🐾 The Walking Whale

In 1992, a **paleontologist** named Hans Thewissen discovered the first fossil of a whale in Pakistan which was, at the time, about 49 million years old. This fossil was of an animal called *Ambulocetus natans*, which had four legs. They were of an older ancestor or relative of the whale called *Pakicetus*.

On examining the jaw and ear, Thewissen discovered that the fossil resembled the structure of a modern whale and had strong hind limbs. He believed that the whale's ancestors began to evolve into their aquatic lifestyle nearly 50 million years ago.

🏅 Incredible Individuals

Hans Thewissen is a Dutch paleontologist and a researcher in the field of anatomy. He focuses on the study of whale fossils to understand how they evolved from land animals. He is also involved in the conservation of beluga whales and does fieldwork in Asia, Alaska, and the neighbouring regions.

Mammalian Orders

Modern mammals are a diverse set. They may share common features, but they are different from each other. This could be due to environmental adaptations. The small shrew, the large elephant, the carnivorous tiger, and the intelligent ape are all mammals.

Classification of Mammals

Scientists have classified mammals into several groups. Each group consists of animals bearing characteristics that are largely similar to each other. This classification, based on newer research, is subject to change.

 01

Monotremes (order Monotremata)
Identifier: Egg-laying mammals
Characteristics: These mammals lay eggs instead of giving birth to young ones.
Example: Duck-billed platypus

 02

Marsupials (infraclass Marsupialia)
Identifier: Pouched animals
Characteristics: These mammals give birth to their young in the abdominal pouch. Their gestation period is short, and the young one is born as an immature foetus that lives in the pouch until it develops fully.
Example: Kangaroo

 **03**

Even-toed Ungulates (order Cetartiodactyla)
Identifier: Even-toed mammals
Characteristics: The group includes land-dwelling even-toed ungulates like camels, deers, cattle, hippopotamuses. Marine mammals like whales and dolphins also belong to this group.
Example: Deer

 04

Cetaceans (infraorder Cetacea)
Identifier: Aquatic mammals
Characteristics: These mammals are quite unique as they are aquatic, have dorsal fins, flippers in the front, and **blubber** and **blowholes**. They are closely related to hippopotami.
Examples: Dolphin

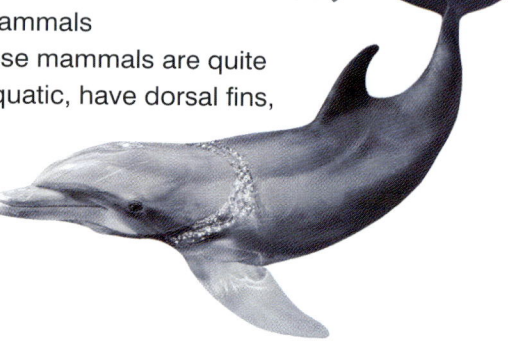

 05

Carnivores (order Carnivora)
Identifier: Flesh-eaters
Characteristics: Carnivorous mammals have large canine teeth and blade-like molars. Most such mammals live on land. Some carnivores are domesticated.
Example: Fox, cat, walrus

06

Pinnipeds (suborder Pinnipedia)
Identifier: Fin-footed
Characteristics: A subgroup of carnivores called 'pinnipeds' live in the water. Their feet have evolved into flippers for swimming.
Example: Seal

 07

Bats (order Chiroptera)
Identifier: Flying mammals
Characteristics: Bats are the only mammals who are capable of true flight. Membranes stretch between the fingers of their hands. They use echolocation (sonar echoes) to navigate.
Example: Vampire Bat

08 Lagomorphs (order Lagomorpha)
Identifier: Hare-shaped
Characteristics: These mammals have long ears, short tails, and hind legs adapted to bouncing movements.
Example: Rabbit

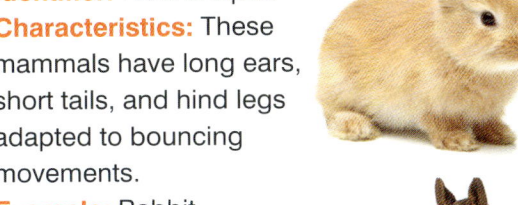

09 Odd-toed Ungulates (order Perissodactyla)
Identifier: Odd-toed and hoofed
Characteristics: They are herbivores with an odd number of toes. They consume food by grazing or **browsing**.
Example: Horse

10 Xenarthrans (Superorder Xenarthra)
Identifier: Toothless mammals
Characteristics: Different species have underdeveloped or no molar teeth. They do not have incisors. They dig the ground and eat insects. Their spines are rigid.
Example: Armadillo

11 Colugo (order Dermoptera)
Identifier: Gliding mammals
Characteristics: Dermoptera are also called flying lemurs or colugos. These mammals glide from tree to tree.
Example: Ring-tailed lemur

12 Primates (order Primates)
Identifier: Big-brained
Characteristics: They have large brains, good vision, and dexterous hands. Many even have **opposable thumbs**.
Example: Chimpanzee

13 Aardvarks (order Tubulidentata)
Identifier: Tubular teeth
Characteristics: They are nocturnal and termite-eating mammals.
Example: Aardvark

14 Rodents (order Rodentia)
Identifier: Largest order of mammals
Characteristics: They are small herbivores with sharp incisors. There are 1,500 living species of rodents.
Example: Squirrel

15 Insectivores (order Eulipotyphla)
Identifier: Insect-eaters
Characteristics: They eat insects and have snouts. They have a good sense of smell and live in burrows or trees.
Example: Hedgehog

16 Pangolins (order Pholidata)
Identifier: Scaly mammals
Characteristics: There are only eight pangolin species alive today. They are covered with scales, and eat ants and termites.
Example: Tree hyrax

17 Hyraxes (order Hyracoidea)
Identifier: Diurnal or nocturnal
Characteristics: These animals are small hooved and have a rodent-like appearance. They are herbivores. While other hoofed animals use their incisors to crop their food, the rock hyraxes use their molars.
Example: Tree hyrax

18 Sirenians (order Sirenia)
Identifier: Aquatic herbivores
Characteristics: TThey live in the waters of tropical and sub-tropical regions. They have front flippers and no hind limbs. These slow mammals eat underwater plants. There are five surviving species of this order.
Example: Manatee

19 Elephants (order Proboscidea)
Identifier: Trunk-nosed mammals
Characteristics: All mammals belonging to this order have trunks. They grab food and drink water using their trunks. They are large herbivorous mammals that graze and browse food.
Example: African elephant

The Carnivore at the Top

Mammalian predators hunt and eat flesh. For this purpose, they need sharp teeth to tear down the meat. Such animals are called carnivores. Polar bears, lions, killer whales, tigers, and wolves are predators. Few mammals such as coyotes are scavengers as well, which means they eat the meat of animals hunted by others. Polar bears are the world's largest terrestrial carnivores.

◀ Polar bears have no fear of other animals as they do not have any natural predators

◀ Less than 2 per cent of polar bear hunts are successful

Habitat

Polar bears are found in countries surrounding the Arctic Circle near the North Pole. They live in Greenland, Canada, Russia, and Norway. Polar bears are not found in Antarctica. Instead, they roam around the vast empty ice fields of the Arctic in search of food.

Size

Polar bears have long necks, short heads, and short tails which are about 7–13 cm long. They are hefty and strong animals who are at the top of the food chain in their habitat.

⊛ Incredible Individuals

Imagine that your friends had never heard of the polar bear. How would you describe it to them? The first recorded sighting of a polar bear was made by William Burrough (1537–1598), who was a navigator from Europe. He, along with the members on his ship *Serchthrift*, witnessed a hunting party chase a polar bear. Another explorer, John Davis (1550–1605), described them as a 'monstrous bigness'. Nearly two centuries later, a man named Constantine John Phipps (1744–1792) described the bears in detail and gave them their scientific name, *Ursus maritimus,* (which translates to sea bear), in his 1774 account *A Voyage Towards the North Pole*.

Trapping Warmth

Polar bears live in the freezing Arctic, so they need to keep themselves warm. They have thick fur in the form of long, hollow hair for insulation. Also, their bodies are covered with a thick layer of fat called blubber that protects them from the harsh winters. While their fur is white, their skin is black and absorbs heat.

Keen Smell

Polar bears have a keen sense of smell. They use it to hunt seals, their favourite prey. It is said that polar bears can smell as far as 9 kilometres away. Once they find a seal's breathing hole, that it creates to come out of the water and breathe, they wait patiently for hours for the seal to emerge so that they can attack it.

Isn't It Amazing!

Kodiak bears get their name from the island of Kodiak where they have lived for the last 12,000 years. The Kodiak archipelago is near Alaska. These bears are a subspecies of the grizzly bears. There are close to 3,500 Kodiak bears surviving today. Fortunately, the bears, living in an unspoiled atmosphere with abundant fish to eat, are showing stable numbers. They are omnivores, and often eat grasses and berries. Young Kodiak bears stay with their cubs for three years.

▲ Polar bears are also called sea bears for their swimming prowess

Swimming Champions

In one hour, polar bears can swim up to 10 km. Unlike all other four-legged animals, they only use their front limbs to swim. They can swim continuously for hours and have even been known to swim hundreds of kilometres without stopping. But these bears are unsuccessful when it comes to hunting in the open waters. That is why they need to look for seals' breathing holes. When they are swimming under water, they close their nostrils and the blubber keeps them warm.

Eating Habits

Polar bears eat seals but they also eat small mammals, birds, bird eggs, and even plants. This is because they are omnivores.

Giving Birth

Polar bears have a long gestation period that lasts around 195–265 days. Female polar bears give birth to young ones in the winter. After they mate, female polar bears try to gain at least 200 kg in weight as that is necessary for them to successfully give birth. They birth the young ones in snow dens which protect the mother and cub from the cold winters.

Female bears dig the dens; they are long tunnels with a narrow entrance. A female polar bear will give birth once in three years. They mostly have twins, while single cubs and triplets are less common. Cubs barely weigh around 680 grams when born. They are weak and have their eyes closed. The mother nurses them with its four mammary glands. Once winter is over, the bear family surfaces from the den. Cubs stay with their mothers for about two years to learn how to become independent.

Not So Good News

Polar bears move from one ice floe (floating ice sheet) to another when they hunt for seals. With rapid climatic changes taking place, often there is not much ice in the Arctic during summers. With so much ice melting, the bears (although they are good swimmers) must swim long distances between floes. Thus, exhausted polar bears drown before reaching their destination. Polar bears are in the International Union for Conservation of Nature (IUCN) list of vulnerable animals and their biggest enemy is climate change and human beings who hunt them.

The Killer Whale

Though they live in the water, the killer whales, or orcas, are some of the most fierce and predatory animals on the Earth. With a large, powerful build that supports a top speed of 56 kmph, and a smart, cunning mind, the killer whale is very well named.

Meet the Killer Whale

Killer whales are also called orcas. Do not be confused by the name though, because they are technically dolphins. These giant carnivores are around 20–26 feet in size and 6,000–10,000 kilograms in weight. They are so large and fierce that they do not have a natural predator. The biggest threat to their existence is human beings.

Appearance

Imagine that you have lost a tooth, but it does not grow back again. That is what happens to killer whales. They only have one set of teeth which are large and interlocking. Killer whales have 40–56 teeth; each is about 7.6 centimetres long. They are sharp and can tear apart the prey easily.

The black and white skin of killer whales is constantly renewed. Therefore, they have very smooth skin that helps them swim fast. They have 7.6-10 centimetre thick layer of blubber beneath their skin.

Diet

Killer whales do not chew their food, they swallow it whole. They eat sea lions, small seals, penguins, walruses, squids, sharks, and fish. Orcas eat about 230 kilograms of food daily.

▲ *Orcas stick to family groups called 'pods'*

Predatory Nature

Killer whales do not have the playful nature that their cousins—the dolphins—are famous for. They might be smart and social like dolphins, but they are also dangerous—one of the top predators of the sea. They live in large pods or family groups. All members of the pod participate in hunting. They hunt using strategies very similar to wolves, such as encircling the prey before moving in for the kill.

Killer whales have black backs, but their stomachs are white. So, a seal sitting on an ice floe might not see the whale, because the black blends well with the water.

They sneak up on and bump off the seal from the floe, into the water, to catch it. Similarly, a fish might not see the white underside as it blends with the light streaming down in the sea from the surface.

◀ *Killer whales also eat krill to maintain their body weight*

The Intelligent Dolphins

Dolphins are warm-blooded mammals and not fish, despite living under water. They belong to the family of cetaceans—a group that also includes porpoises, orcas, and whales. Most dolphins have a small build of around 6.2-8.2 feet. They have streamlined bodies, a pointed snout, and sharp teeth.

Behaviour

Dolphins are remarkably intelligent and playful marine mammals.

They are predominantly found in shallow waters of tropical or temperate regions. Just like bats, they use echolocation to navigate the waters and hunt for fish, squids, and crustaceans. To conserve energy, dolphins bow-ride and swim alongside ships. They are known for their grace and playfulness.

▲ *Dolphins bow-riding with a boat*

A Dolphin at Rest

Unlike human beings, who can breathe subconsciously, dolphins have to consciously take air into their lungs. They do not have gills, like fish. Instead, they breathe through a blowhole, which is a nostril located on top of their heads. When dolphins sleep, one part of their brain switches off, while the other remains alert to keep breathing. They switch sides in approximately two hours and the other part of the brain wakes up, watching for predators and signalling when to come up for fresh air. This is called catnapping. Individual dolphins enter into a deeper form of sleep, usually in the night, called logging. This name comes from the fact that a dolphin looks like a log floating in the water while it is in deep sleep.

Smiling Dolphins

Bottlenose dolphins are amongst the most popular dolphin species and commonly perform at oceanariums because of their great communication abilities. If you look at this dolphin's face, it looks like it is always smiling because of the curvature of its mouth. Every dolphin has a unique whistling sound. Bottlenose dolphins can remember and recognise the sound of each dolphin, even after they are separated for 10 to 20 years.

Parenting

Female dolphins sleep on the move so that they can take care of the young by towing them along in their slipstream. This is called echelon swimming. Baby dolphins need a lot of rest and sleep and will drown if their mother does not carry them to the surface. While looking after newborns, the mothers cannot sleep for weeks at a time as baby dolphins are not born with enough blubber to keep them afloat. They stay with their mothers till they are eight years old. Dolphins also travel in pairs and sleep while slowly swimming with each other.

▲ *The 'smiling' bottlenose dolphin*

◀ *Dolphins can live in groups of as few as five and as many as hundreds. They are social learners*

Predators of the Night

▶ Some bats can achieve flight speeds of up to 160 kmph

Bats are commonly mistaken for birds because they can fly, but they are mammals. They emerge at night and sleep during the day. These flying mammals come in varied sizes; the tiniest one being the bumblebee bat, with a wing span of up to 17 centimetres. Many species of bats live on fruits, while vampire bats drink the blood of other animals.

Vampire Bats

Vampire bats rest in caves, hollows of trees, and abandoned buildings. They live in Mexico, Central America, and South America. These mammals live in groups ranging from 100 to 1,000.

Vampire bats have a lifespan of about 12 years. They are small, with a length of 7 or 9 centimetres and a weight of about 15–45 grams.

A Bloody Affair

Unlike the mythical creatures they are named after, vampire bats do not suck blood. They make a small cut on their prey with their teeth and drink the blood that flows out. Theses bats are so agile that at times they can drink blood from an animal or bird for 30 minutes before waking them up. The prey is not harmed, but might get infections.

▲ Most bats hang upside down while resting

Vampire bats usually drink blood from pigs, cows, horses and birds. These bats have important adaptations which help them in feeding. They have a heat sensor on their nose which helps them find warm blood flowing through the victim. While feeding, their saliva prevents blood from clotting. The young vampire bats do not drink blood but feed on their mother's milk instead for almost three months after birth. They cling to the mother even while she is in flight.

Echolocation

Bats have very small eyes and extremely sensitive sight. They cannot see colours like human beings, but they can see in the dark. As they hunt at night, vampire bats also use **echolocation**. It means that bats send sound waves with their mouth or nose. These bounce off on surfaces like the walls of a cave and echo back to the bat. The signal is enough for it to identify a prey (its size or location) and any hurdles.

Incredible Individuals

An Italian scientist named Lazzaro Spallanzani (1729–1799) discovered that bats were able to navigate through hurdles and find their prey even if they were blinded. He made several discoveries about how the bodies of bats function and how they reproduce.

ANIMALS | MAMMALS

The Prowling Tiger

There are many species of tigers, with the Bengal tigers being one of the most famous ones. They can be easily spotted because of their bright orange-reddish coats with unique dark stripes. They are found in very diverse habitats such as tropical forests, grasslands, swamps, rocky terrains, and even colder regions like Siberia.

Behaviour

Tigers are the biggest cats in the big cat family that includes leopards, lions, and cheetahs. They have three-foot long tails which allow them to maintain balance. On average, they weigh between 100 to 350 kilograms, stand around 3 feet tall and have sharp claws. The mammals use their claws to swiftly kill their prey.

Tigers are solitary hunters. Their agility makes them very dangerous. They usually prey on deer, antelopes, pigs, water buffaloes, and even horses. They are mostly nocturnal mammals that hunt every 4–7 days and can eat up to 10 kilograms of meat in one sitting. Tigers always know when they are in another tiger's territory because they mark their territories with their urine or by scratching the nearby trees.

▲ Tigers are great swimmers. The Bengal tiger cools off by taking a quick swim and splashes around in the water

A Tiger's Roar

In the early 1900s, there were over 100,000 tigers roaming around in their territories, but today their numbers have reduced greatly. Tigers are now considered to be an endangered species. They have dwindled in population primarily because of poaching, hunting, and loss of habitat. Today, not more than 4,000 tigers exist in the world.

▶ White or bleached tigers are seen in India. They are quite rare. They are not a separate species from Bengal tigers, but just have a different pigmentation

▼ Tigers are often hunted for their skin and teeth

Species	Status
Bengal tiger	Less than 2,000
Indochinese tiger	Around 350
Siberian/Amur tiger	Around 500
Sumatran tiger	Less than 400
Malayan tiger	Less than 200
South Chinese tiger	Extinct in the wild; bred in captivity
Caspian tiger	Extinct
Javan tiger	Extinct
Bali tiger	Extinct

The Agile Fox

Foxes do not hunt in packs, unlike their wolf cousins. Instead, they hunt extra prey and bury it away for later. This behaviour has probably contributed to their 'sly' reputation. The fox is popularly mentioned in legends where it is portrayed primarily as cunning or intelligent. The male fox is called reynard and the female fox, vixen. Foxes belong to the larger canine family called Canidae, of which dogs are also a part.

Special Features

Though they are related to dogs, foxes have cat-like retractable claws and vertical pupils. They have a slender frame, thin legs, a pointed nose, and a bushy tail. Grey foxes are the only canines that can climb trees to escape attackers.

Foxes easily adapt to numerous kinds of habitats and exist in every continent except Antarctica. They use their nocturnal abilities to hunt mice, birds, frogs, insects, fruits, and seeds, as they are omnivores.

▶ The artic or polar fox uses its white fur to camouflage itself in the snow against predators

▼ Red foxes can be very agile, jumping to even 7 feet to cross a fence

The Red Fox

There are 37 types of foxes, but the red fox is the most common. Its natural habitat can range from arid deserts to the Arctic tundra. They are spotted in Australia and Central America. Red foxes are small creatures, generally about 90–105 centimetres long, of which 35-40 cm is the tail and weigh just 5–7 kilograms. This is the same weight as that of a one-year-old baby.

Red foxes have adapted so well to the human environment that they are now considered pets in Australia. They can be found in woods, farmlands, and many large suburbs.

What Does the Fox Say?

Foxes seem to have a lot to talk about. They are extremely vocal animals, and have at least 28 different types of calls, 8 of which are only used by their cubs.

Contact call: It is made by two foxes as they approach each other. It sounds similar to a dog's bark, but is of a higher pitch, like an owl's hoot. Once the foxes make physical contact, they have a greeting call that sounds like a chicken's clucking.

Interaction call: These sounds vary based on social status and how aggressive the fox is. A submissive fox will let out a high-pitched whine when facing an aggressive fox. They also make a clicking sound called gekkering when they are feeling playful or aggressive.

Alarm call: These are made by parents to warn each other about oncoming danger. It sounds like a sharp 'waaaah'. The vixen's scream is another terrifying and loud sound made in anguish.

The Galloping Horse

Horses belong to the Equidae family. They comprise a singular species called *Equus caballus*. There are many different breeds within this species. Horses are a common sight because human beings have domesticated them and used them as means of transportation for centuries. A male horse is called a stallion and a female horse is called a mare. Young horses are known as foals.

Features

Horses are animals of speed. They have long, firm legs with hooves they use to gallop. Their compact bodies are supported by the tips of their toes, allowing their limbs to extend forward and gain speed. They have large and complex brains in their well-rounded skulls. This allows for great muscle coordination.

Horses weigh between 350–1,000 kilograms. As they are herbivores, they have a set of sharp, high-crowned teeth that they use to graze and grind grass. Horses also have long digestive tracts to digest cellulose from vegetation. Their diet consists of hay, grain and water. They need sugar and lots of salt, which they can get from vegetables and fruits.

Behaviour

Horses have developed sensory systems for good memory, accurate judgement and strong instincts. They are social herd animals. Their intrinsic nature is to actively seek out a mutually beneficial relationship. They do not fare well in isolation. Human beings have exploited this trait and domesticated them for centuries. Horses scare easily and only get aggressive when they are mistreated or cannot flee.

In Real Life

Horses have played a very important role in human civilisation for centuries now. They were used by kings and soldiers in combat and warfare. They routinely feature in art as steady companions for human beings. For centuries, human beings have been heavily reliant on these animals for transportation. Literature often depicts horses as the vehicle of choice for noble heroes and the gods. Today, riding horses has become a recreational sport. Horses are also at the centre of various sports from polo to horse racing, and were used for jousting in the medieval era. They were also used to make glue as they, among other animals, contain a lot of collagen, a protein found in connective tissue, hide, and bone. It is evident that horses and humans go a long way back.

How Do Horses Sleep?

Human beings tend to sleep at a stretch for eight hours. Horses do not do this. They rest for short periods, many times a day. Their sleeping patterns change depending upon their age and the weather. They cannot sleep well in the cold. Till the age of three months, young foals spend half their day sleeping by lying down. As they grow older, they sleep standing up. For adult horses, lying down can be more challenging than standing, so they only lie down for a short time.

▶ Horses need about three hours of sleep each day

▼ Horses have strong instincts that allow them to sense distant danger. They can even sense the emotional temperament of their riders

The Graceful Deer

Reindeers have often been associated with Christmas tales, and are well-known all over the world. They belong to the deer family. Except for Australia and Antarctica, deers are native to every continent. They are noted for having two large and two small hooves on each foot. Male deers have strong antlers in most species, while only female reindeers have antlers. They shed and regrow these antlers every year. Deers also have scent glands on their legs but do not have rectal or vulval glands; they do not have a gall bladder either.

Diet

Since deer have very complex digestive organs, they are very specialised herbivores. They feed on grasses, fruits, aquatic plants, and herbs that contain protein and are easily digestible. Due to this limitation, they cannot sustain themselves in deserts, dry grasslands, or leached faunas. Deer have learnt to identify disturbed ecosystems and use it to their advantage. If there has been a flood, a wildfire, or an avalanche, they exploit the nutrient-rich landscape the disaster leaves in its wake.

Behaviour

Deer belonging to different sets of fauna differ in their survival tactics. Those who belong to forests can easily hide in the thick of the forest. Those who belong to a flat terrain tend to be specialised runners and can bolt at the sign of danger. Deer who live on rocky terrains tend to be specialised jumpers and can explore high altitudes that are inaccessible to their predators.

▼ *Deer are seen as gentle animals, often skittish and nervous around predators. If they sense danger, they take off running*

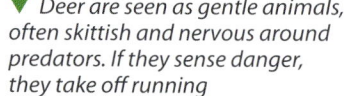

Reindeers

Also referred to as caribou, reindeer live in the far northern regions of North America, Europe, and Asia. They are found in the Arctic tundra and nearby forests. They are the most domesticated species of deer, often used as pets and to pull sleighs in the snow. The antlers of male reindeer can grow up to 4.3 feet, making them look magnificent. They are exceptional swimmers and their coats are well-insulated. Their cloven hoofs are deep and thus, they are able to walk on soft ground and snow.

▲ *Reindeer's noses are specially designed to warm the air before it reaches their lungs*

Isn't It Amazing!

During harsh winters, reindeers survive on a particular lichen due to a lack of vegetation. They supplement this by recycling urea, which is normally a waste product. They do it within their digestive system by using up all the nitrogen present in the urea. Males shed their antlers during such periods, but females keep them throughout winter to defend themselves from other deer trying to share their food.

The Unique Rodents

Rodents are the largest group of mammals, having over 2,050 living species. They have 27 separate families such as porcupines, mice, beavers, and squirrels, among others. They are characterised by their rootless incisor teeth which are coated with thick enamel. They eat their food by gnawing, and thus their teeth have very chiselled edges. Rodents have to keep gnawing as their incisor teeth never stop growing.

Size

Rodents are small creatures. The largest living one is the capybara, which weighs around 35-66 kilograms on average. Most rodents do not live longer than a year, but some of the larger ones, like beavers, live almost till they are 20 years of age. As a result of their short lifespans, they have very fast reproductive cycles and achieve sexual maturity very quickly.

▲ *Capybaras are extremely friendly; they interact with about every other animal*

Diet

The dietary behaviour of rodents changes according to the species. Their preferences can be set apart using various classifications such as diet patterns, and hunting or gathering styles. Rodents may be herbivorous or omnivorous. They have species which might live an adaptable lifestyle of being hunters as the opportunity presents itself, or being specialists e.g. the grasshopper mouse hunts arthropods, while some rodents hunt vertebrates.

Beavers

Beavers are the second-largest rodents with bodies extending up to 120 cm. They are primarily nocturnal and amphibious creatures that live in rivers, streams, marshes, and ponds. They have short legs and a stout body with a small, broad, and blunt head. As herbivores, their diet consists mostly of bark, leaves, twigs, roots, and aquatic plants.

▲ *Mice live close to their food source and build colonies near human homes. Their rapid growth in population can prove to be quite tiresome for human beings*

Mice

A mouse is a small nocturnal mammal with a pointed snout, small rounded ears, and an almost hairless tail which can grow as long as its body. Mice have poor eyesight but a keen sense of smell and hearing. There are more than 30 known species of these rodents. The house mouse is a popular pet and other mouse species seen in and around the house are the field mouse, the American white-footed mouse, and the deer mouse. They are widely hunted by cats, wild dogs, foxes, birds of prey, and snakes. In their natural habitat mice are herbivores that eat all kinds of fruit and grains from plants. Using their whiskers to sense changes in temperature, mice build winding burrows with many escape routes.

◄ *Beavers can use their incisors to block the water from entering their mouth as they cut branches growing under the water's surface*

The Herbivorous Hippo

A hippopotamus looks aggressive and strong, so it is often thought to be a carnivore, but it is herbivorous. Herbivores eat grass and leaves. Mammals like giraffes, cows, elephants, sheep, and goats are some more examples of herbivores. These animals have flat and wide molar teeth to grind the grasses and leaves, unlike predators who need sharp canine teeth to cut and bite into flesh.

Aggressive Hippos

Hippopotamuses look docile, slow, and sluggish, but they can get aggressive when they feel threatened. On land, they can run at the speed of 15 kmph and even reach a speed of 30 kmph for short distances. There have been incidents when they have killed buffaloes, impalas, as well as human beings. Even a ferocious predator like a lion cannot take on a hippo on its own and needs to hunt it in pairs.

Habitat

Hippopotamuses look for food on land, but water is essential to their habitats. In fact, their name translates to 'river horse'. Once, they were found all over Africa, but are now confined to some parts of East and West Africa. Due to habitat loss and hunting, they are now listed as a vulnerable species.

Size

Hippopotamuses have barrel-shaped bodies, short legs and tails, and large heads. Their skin can be greyish or brownish, with blotches of faded pink on the underside. They can weigh as much as around 3,000 kilograms, making them the second-largest terrestrial animal living in the world.

Cooling Effect

Hippopotamuses stay in places with hot climates. To cool themselves off, they spend their days in rivers and lakes. Interestingly, they produce a natural substance that acts like suntan lotion when they sweat. It is an oily red liquid which protects their skin from the Sun and prevents drying.

Herds

Hippopotamuses live in groups of ten or twenty. The herd has a dominant male who is protective of the group. The others in the herd are the females, young ones, and non-breeding males. To keep other males away, male hippopotamuses open their mouth wide to display their long, razor-sharp canines. They are also known to make loud noises and splash aggressively in water. Female hippos, also known as cows, give birth to a single calf every two years. They stick to their herd as it offers protection against predators such as crocodiles and lions.

◄ *The hippopotamus is considered to be the most dangerous animal in Africa*

The Strong Elephant

Elephants are the largest terrestrial animals on Earth. They are known for their distinctively long noses or trunks, large; floppy ears; and wide, thick legs. The two major types of elephants, the Asian elephant and the African elephant inhabit separate continents.

Diet

Their diet consists of grasses, roots, fruits, and bark. They use their tusks to pull the bark from trees and dig roots out of the ground. These giants spend a majority of their day feeding. An adult can eat 136 kg of food in a day.

Reproduction

Male elephants are referred to as 'bulls' and females as 'cows'. Post copulation, the cow's period of gestation is around 22 months. When the baby elephant is finally delivered, it can weigh around 91 kilograms and stand 3 feet tall. A baby elephant is called a 'calf'. The calf gains 1 kilogram every day up until it is one year old. By the time they are two years old, calves are ready to be weaned. Male calves leave, while females stay with the herd.

▼ African elephants are the largest land animals in the world

▲ Young elephants have no survival instinct; they rely on their mothers completely

Asian Elephant	African Elephant
Asian elephants grow up to 6.5-11.5 feet from shoulder to toe and weigh 2,500–5,500 kilograms.	African elephants can grow 8.2–13 feet from shoulder to toe and weigh 4,000-7,000 kilograms.
They live in Nepal, India, and Southeast Asia in scrub forests and rainforests.	These elephants inhabit sub-Saharan Africa, the rain forests of Central and West Africa, and the Sahel desert in Mali.
These elephants have smaller, round ears.	They have much larger ears shaped a bit like the continent of Africa.
Asian elephants have twin-domed heads, which means there is a divot line running up the head.	African elephants have rounded heads.

Behaviour

A group of elephants is called a herd. It is led by a matriarch, which is the oldest female. The matriarch is known to train the calves on how to behave amongst the community, which is a strong, close-knit family. Females, as well as young and old elephants stick together in a herd. Adult males tend to wander on their own.

Elephants display many strong emotions and instincts like empathy, mischief, and mourning. They sometimes hug by wrapping their trunks together in displays of greeting and affection or even respect, as taught by the matriarch. Elephants also use their distinctive trunks to help lift or nudge an elephant calf over an obstacle or to pull them out from a mud pit.

◄ Asian elephant

All About Marsupials

Similar to other mammals, marsupials have hair and mammary glands. Over 250 species of marsupials exist. They are characterised by the continued development and maternal dependency of their newborns.

▲ Baby kangaroos are known as joeys

Young Marsupials

The young are very vulnerable at the time of their birth and are heavily reliant on the mother's milk. They fasten their mouth firmly on the mother's swollen up teats, and continue to develop for months in her marsupium. The marsupium or the pouch is a flap of skin that covers the mother's lower abdomen and teats. After a few months of warmth and shelter in the mother's pouch, the baby is gradually weaned off.

The Anteater

If you see an anteater, you will wonder how this toothless, strange-looking animal functions. They have a very long, worm-like tongue that helps them gulp down termites and ants easily. They have a tube-like snout and powerful, big claws that can tear down strong anthills. Their eyes and ears are small and rounded and they have very poor eyesight and hearing. Their brain is round and small too. But it is interesting how the anteaters' sense of smell is considered to be 40 times stronger than that of human beings! They live in tropical grasslands and forests in Central and South America. Anteaters easily eat a few thousand ants in one sitting and then abandon the nest. The biggest species are over 40 kilograms.

Isn't It Amazing!

The modern kangaroo is a herbivore. Can you imagine a kangaroo that eats flesh? There was an extinct marsupial called *Ekaltadeta* closely related to the cute, jumpy kangaroos of today. They are also known as the killer kangaroo. As big as the modern dog, these killer kangaroos had large teeth and held down their prey with their front legs.

▲ The biggest species of anteaters is the giant anteater

Koala

Koalas, also referred to as koala bears, are not bears, but are marsupials. They live in Australia on eucalyptus trees. They can eat more than a pound of leaves in a day. Mind you, they are fussy eaters and only choose the best leaves. They do not drink much water as they get all the water they need from the leaves they eat. The animals sleep more than 18 hours a day. A koala baby, when born is called the joey, and is blind and earless.

Kangaroos

Kangaroos are large animals that hop from place to place, at speeds as high as 56 kmph. They travel far and wide in search of food and water. These mammals have a pouch in which they carry their joey and belong to the *Macropodidae* family of marsupials that includes the happy quokkas and wallaroos.

▲ Koalas eat up to 1 kg of eucalyptus leaves every day

The Playful Seal

Seals belong to a species of web-footed aquatic mammals found in frigid water bodies. They have been known to live for more than 30 years. Some seals even make caves of snow to live in, while others never leave the ice pack and poke breathing holes in the ice. They are elegant and brisk swimmers owing to their structure, which has a rounded middle that tapers toward the ends.

Classification

There are two types of seals classified according to whether they have ears or are earless: True seals and eared seals. True seals are earless, while the eared seals comprise the sea lions and fur seals who have ears. Seals are carnivores, eating mainly fish, though some also consume squid, other molluscs, and crustaceans.

▲ A seal's whiskers help in detecting prey in dark, murky waters

True seals are more streamlined than fur seals and sea lions, and can therefore swim more effectively over long distances. However, because they cannot turn their hind flippers downwards, they are very clumsy on land, having to wriggle with their front flippers and abdominal muscles. This method of locomotion is called galumphing.

Migration of Elephant Seals

There are two types of elephant seals; the northern and the southern. The southern ones live in Antarctica, while the northern ones are seen on rocky beaches of northern oceans. It is there that they **moult**, sleep, mate, and give birth to young ones. However, the beaches are not their permanent abodes, in fact they spend more time in the ocean. These seals are known to migrate. They go migrating into the northern Pacific Ocean in the hunt for food, which gives them enough energy reserves for land-based activities. Interestingly, the male and female elephant seals like to migrate separately. Males travel nearly 21,000 kilometres in one year, while females travel almost 18,000 kilometres. Males fast for four months while they are on land and females fast for two months. All these different schedules make for a complicated migration season!

▲ Elephant seals can hold their breath for over 100 minutes

Social Beings

Seals are social animals that gather in large groups on beaches or masses of ice for the purpose of breeding. Male seals are called 'bulls', females are known as 'cows', and the baby seals are called 'pups'. Usually, seals form pairs during the period of procreation but some exceptions exist amongst the species. The gestation period lasts about 11 months. They give birth in dugouts of snow or on the open ice. The mother is known to stay out of water and not feed while she nurses the pup. The offspring acquire weight rapidly and stay on land till their waterproof fur grows.

On the Decline

Seals are hunted by killer whales, polar bears, leopard seals, large sharks, and human beings. Their species have seen a severe and rapid decrease in numbers in recent years. Many factors, including overfishing of other species, shooting by fishermen, and pollution have contributed to the decline.

◀ Cape fur seals are often seen nibbling on rocks

The Intelligent Primates

Scientists are known to have studied the teeth of primates to make findings about them. Around 57 million years ago, there lived a mammal which was probably the first true primate to have ever lived. It was a small animal named *'Altiatlasius'*. Its fossil was discovered in Morocco. Scientists feel it could be an important link in the evolution of primates.

What are Primates?

▶ *Some trainers have managed to train chimpanzees to perform sign language as part of an experiment*

A primate is mammalian group which includes monkeys, lemurs, tarsiers, apes, and human beings. Primates have big brains and are intelligent animals. Their eyes look straight ahead from their face.

Each of their hands has five fingers and each hind limb or foot has five toes. Primates are dexterous, meaning they can use their hands skilfully. Some ape species and human beings even have opposable thumbs.

▲ *An adult pygmy marmoset weighs only about 100 grams*

World's Smallest Monkey

It is the pygmy marmoset. It is so small that it can fit in the human palm and is found mainly in Brazil, Peru, and Colombia. These monkeys can leap up to 5 metres and can turn their heads backwards.

These adaptations help the pygmy marmoset scan the surroundings for predators. An interesting feature of this monkey is that while it is in conversation with others of its kind, it waits for its turn to speak.

World's Loudest Monkey

How loud can the howler monkeys be? When they shout, you can hear them even from 5 kilometres away! Howler monkeys shout to let others know where their territory is. One group shouts as a call, and in return, the second group answers.

Howler monkeys shout early in the morning and in the evening. They live on treetops and have tails that can grip branches of trees.

◀ *Howler monkeys live in groups where the dominant male has the loudest shout*

▶ *Tarsier babies are the largest as compared to their mothers*

Shy Primates

Tarsiers, with their spooky eyes, are said to bring bad luck by villagers in Borneo. They frighten many with their appearance. These small monkeys are residents of Southeast Asia. Their striking feature is their remarkably huge eyes that they use to see better at night, as they are nocturnal animals. This might be because they lack the tapetum, a reflective layer present in most nocturnal animals, which helps them see in low light. They can rotate their heads 180 degrees and have long ankle bones. They are the only entirely carnivorous primates and they feed on insects, lizards, and snakes.

ANIMALS | MAMMALS | 25

Sun Soakers

Found in Madagascar and a few neighbouring islands, the ring-tailed lemurs are great sunbathers. Every morning, they sit on the ground with their arms open wide, facing the Sun. These animals live in groups of 15–20.

A ring-tailed lemur has a long, striped, black and white tail. The animals mainly eat fruits. They have powerful scent glands, which they use to mark their territory, communicate, and attack predators.

◀ *Ring-tailed lemurs look for food together. After eating, they like to relax in spots that receive sunlight*

Close Cousins

Chimpanzees are probably the closest relatives of human beings in the primate family, apart from bonobos. These primate species reside in the tropical forests of Africa and are omnivores. They are extremely intelligent, with logical thinking and problem-solving capabilities. Chimpanzees live in groups called communities and are extroverted by nature. They are known to display love and affection towards others. The mother and child, and siblings share strong bonds and, just like human beings, even they can display a bad temper.

Orangutans

'Orangutan' in Malay means 'person of the forest'. This primate is long-haired, orangish in colour, and has an enormous arm span (almost 7 feet in males) when stretched. Orangutans are found in Sumatra and Borneo.

An average orangutan spends most of its life in trees. It makes itself a bed in the tree by breaking apart branches, twigs, and leaves. It makes a new bed every night, and uses large leaves as an umbrella to keep itself dry from the constant tropical rains.

▼ *Orangutans are semi-solitary creatures, which means they like to live around two or three others at a time*

⭐ Incredible Individuals

Jane Goodall is a famous British **ethologist**, who has lived among and studied chimpanzees in Gombe on the shores of Lake Tanganyika. She gave us a lot of insights about chimpanzees, such as that they can make tools and perform many social interactions. She has written a number of books and articles on the subject.

▲ *Jane Goodall started her research without a degree*

Our Evolution

Do you ever wonder how human beings evolved from apes? Going by the knowledge gained so far, we have discovered that human beings are the most skilled and developed mammals in the history of the evolution of Earth. The story of humans started around six million years ago in Africa. Our primate ancestors spent most of their time on trees, just like modern primates. So, what changed?

The Rough Details

It is said that an ancient ancestor of human beings came down from the safety of the trees and began to roam the lands—it is not yet certain if they roamed grasslands or forests. It was probably at this point that humans became different from our closest living relatives, the chimpanzees and other such apes.

Scientists have put the human tribe into a group called 'Hominin'. The modern human beings (called *homo sapiens*) are the only living members of this tribe, but fossil evidence shows that many hominins preceded us. The history spans more than a million years:

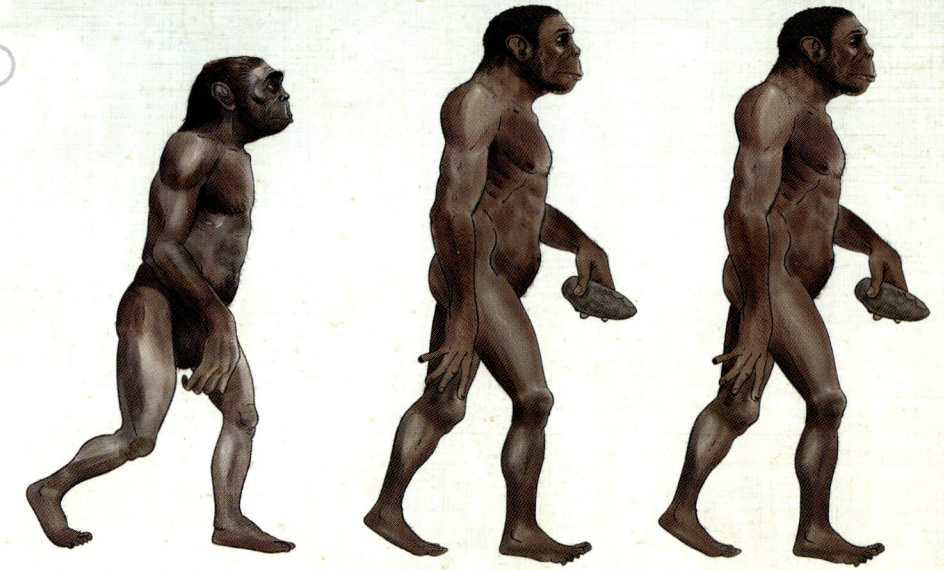

4.4 Million Years Ago

Ardipithecus, so far, is considered the first hominin. While there are ape fossils older than *Ardipithecus,* there is no evidence of them being human ancestors. *Ardipithecus* appeared in forests of present-day Ethiopia. It was probably not a good walker or runner, but its fossils indicate the presence of the same anchors for muscles we have on our pelvis, which chimpanzees and other apes lack.

3 Million Years Ago

Our first true human ancestor, *Australopithecus* appeared in Africa. A female *Australopithecus* was discovered in 1974 in Hadar, Ethiopia. She was named 'Lucy' after a song by the Beatles. The fossil evidence shows that Lucy was a bipedal, which means she walked on two legs. She was seen to have wisdom teeth. *Australopithecus* had a larger and a more complex brain structure.

2 Million Years Ago

Almost 2-million-year-old fossils of *Homo habilis* were discovered in Koobi Fora in Kenya and Olduvai Gorge in Tanzania. The word means 'handy man' or 'hand-using man'. The fossils show that the brain had increased in size and complexity yet again. Scientists feel that *Homo habilis* could use stones as tools. It was the development of such skills that set humans apart in the animal kingdom.

1.7 Million Years Ago

Homo erectus, which refers to the species' relatively erect posture, was the first ancestor to have human-like body proportions. This species first appeared in East Africa and spread to various parts of Africa, Asia, and Europe. Along with the use of stone tools, these early humans discovered fire.

ANIMALS | MAMMALS | 27

Isn't It Amazing!

Did you know humans are mammals with the longest hair? If you did not cut it, your hair would reach the floor and beyond. Beards and moustaches can also grow very long. A close second is the musk oxen, an animal which lives in the Arctic. It has a long, brown coat which reaches almost down to its feet. The Arctic fox has a thick coat of fur which can survive temperatures that drop below -50° C. Its coat turns from white to brown during the cold harsh winter and even grows longer for more protection.

◀ History of humankind (L–R: Ardipithecus, Australopithecus, Homo habilis, Home erectus, Homo neanderthalensis, Homo sapiens)

400,000 Years Ago

Around the time *Homo erectus* was roaming the various continents, a new type of hominin appeared in Europe. They were called *Homo neanderthalensis* or simply Neanderthals, named after the Neander Valley in Germany, where the first fossil was discovered. These are the closest relatives of mankind on the evolutionary map. Their bodies were shorter, and they had larger brains. They also had angular cheek bones and large noses.

Community Living

Neanderthals were the first to exhibit the traits of civilisation. They controlled fire, built shelters, and used stone tools for hunting. They practiced burial rituals for the dead. They were the first to develop art in the form of cave paintings which show their culture, society, and the world they lived in. They disappeared nearly 40,000 years ago. They either assimilated with modern *Homo sapiens* or became extinct.

200,000–100,000 Years Ago

Homo sapiens are thought to have evolved in Africa. The oldest remains unearthed so far are from Morocco. All of us living on planet Earth today belong to this species. *Homo sapiens* have the most complex and largest brain capacities amongst any hominin species. They have an erect posture, light jaws, and small teeth.

Development of Society

Human beings, as they are called, colonised and spread across the different continents on Earth. Our ancestors began the use of complex tools, not just for hunting, but farming as well. They built villages, which created societies. They created art, music, foods, ornaments, clothes, and rituals, which form the basis of human civilisation as we know today.

How Babies Are Born

All living species need to reproduce to survive and exist. Depending upon how the reproduction process takes place, mammals are classified into three main groups—placental, monotremes, and marsupials. The mammals belonging to these three groups also have different ways of nursing their babies.

Placental Mammals

They are the most common mammals in the world as all mammals except monotremes and marsupials are placental. They nourish their unborn babies in the womb through a membrane called **placenta**. The placenta absorbs nutrients and oxygen from the mother's blood. It then passes them onto the foetus through a long cord called the **umbilical cord**. This is the case in most mammals such as tigers, monkeys, elephants, and human beings.

▲ Monkeys only give birth every couple of years

Monotremes

Monotremes are the most ancient living order of mammals. The name means 'single hole'. As the name suggests, monotremes have a single opening for excretion and reproduction. They are egg-laying mammals. They have managed to retain certain physical characteristics that were lost in other mammals.

Another interesting feature of monotremes is that they have low body temperatures like reptiles, unlike the other warm-blooded mammals. The platypus and echidnas (spiny anteaters) are monotremes.

Echidna

Echidnas can be long-beaked or short-beaked. They are covered in spines and have a tubular beak through which they eat and breathe. They are found in New Guinea and Tasmania, Australia.

The female echidna is followed by many male echidnas during the breeding season. At the end of the gestation period, which is 23 days, the female echidna lays an egg in a skin pouch on her belly. She **incubates** the egg for 10 days until it finally hatches. The baby echidna rests in a burrow and drinks milk from the mother's mammary hairs. Once it develops its fur and spines fully, it can leave the burrow and feed itself.

▲ Echidnas are also known as spiny anteaters

In Real Life

Research has found that emperor penguins breed on iceshelves. While some breeds live on sea ice, some are found to also live on the iceshelves. As they rely on the ice, the population of emperor penguins could rapidly decline due to global warming. In these harsh and cold conditions, the female emperor penguin produces a single egg. She doesn't build a nest, rather she has the male keep the egg warm.

▶ An emperor penguin egg weighs around 460 g

ANIMALS | MAMMALS

Duck-billed Platypus

Interestingly, the opposite sexes of the duck-billed platypus only interact with each other to mate when they reach the age of four. The mating process takes place in water. The female platypus usually lays two small eggs after a gestation period of two weeks to one month. She incubates the egg for 6–10 days by curling her body around the eggs until her tail touches her bill.

When the eggs hatch, the young platypuses stay in burrows and suckle milk from the mother's mammary hair. People who first began to take notice and observe this animal thought it had a comical appearance, almost like a duck's beak was sewn onto a random mammal. The duck-billed platypus is certainly one of nature's strangest looking animals.

Marsupials

Like placental mammals, marsupials also have placenta but as it is not properly developed, their gestation period is shorter. The animals in this group have a pouch, but do not lay eggs. The females give birth to very tiny and premature babies. These babies stay in the pouch, feeding on the mother's milk until they grow, develop, and are ready for the world. The Tasmanian devil and opossums are examples of marsupials.

Isn't It Amazing!

The opossum pretends to be dead when it is confronted by a predator! It flops to the ground and rolls its tongue out to the side. It closes its eyes, or makes them look glassy with a vacant, dead stare. It also emits a rancid odour which drives away its predators. Even if its enemy—like a dog or a coyote—decides to jab the motionless body, the opossum remains still. After the predator leaves, the opossum escapes.

Tasmanian Devil

The Tasmanian devil has a short lifespan of eight years. It matures and is ready to mate by the age of two. At one time, a female Tasmanian devil gives birth to two or four young ones. They stop breeding at the age of five. The young ones are bound to the mother or stay in the pouch for 10 months, after which they become independent. They drink milk from the teats in their mother's pouch.

◀ In one week, the birth weight of a baby opossum increases tenfold

▲ Once the Tasmanian devil was found all over Australia, but now it is only found in Tasmania

Opossum

The male opossum is known to be territorial and violent during the mating season. The gestation period is very short, lasting only 12 days after mating. The opossum gives birth to a litter of 16–20 babies, but less than half of them survive. At birth, they are the size of a mosquito! They are blind for the first two months after birth and stay in the safety of the mother's pouch till 75–85 days. They leave their mother when they are three to four months of age.

◀ Common brushtail possums communicate through sound and scent

From Here to There

Migration is the annual movement of animals from one place to another. Animals migrate for better climatic conditions, food, and for the breeding season. Living in one place could reduce the chances of survival for many animals. It is not just birds and insects that migrate. Quite a few mammals also go through periods of migration.

🐾 The Great Migration

Inhabiting the African **savannahs** are the wildebeest. These mammals belong to the antelope family, such as the gazelles. They are known for their annual migration.

Come March, these mammals, with their new calves, leave Serengeti in Tanzania to reach Masai Mara in Kenya. Close to 1.5 million wildebeest travel in an enormous clockwise loop on a year-long trek that spans 1,000 kilometres. They are followed by a few thousand gazelles, impalas and zebras. Scientists are yet to decode the exact reason for this migration; they suspect that a change in the chemical composition of the grass, induced by rains, might be responsible.

In November, they start their trek back to Serengeti. However, the migration is not without its dangers. They not only have to cross rivers filled with crocodiles, but also brave land predators like cheetahs, African dogs, and hyenas. Along the way, they lose approximately 250,000 members.

▲ *Wildebeest are responsible for the largest terrestrial migration in the world*

🐾 Oceanic Journey

Humpback whales are mammals living in the oceans. They weigh around 30,000 kilograms. These mammals follow a long-distance migration pattern, travelling close to 10,000 km every year.

In the polar areas where the humpback whales reside, they eat krill in the summer months. However, in winters, when they migrate, breed, and calve, the animals eat nothing. Instead they survive on blubber or fat stored in their bodies. The humpback whales reside in the Northern hemisphere and migrate to Hawaii, while those in the Southern hemisphere migrate to Eastern Australia.

▲ *Humpback whales have moved from 'vulnerable' to the 'least concerned' category on IUCN's Red List*

💡 Isn't It Amazing!

Male humpback whales are great singers. They create songs in the form of high-pitched squeals and whistles or low gurgles. Their songs can last for 30 minutes. It is said that male humpbacks sing to attract mates in the breeding season. They create a new song for each new breeding season, which is picked by many others in the area, making it the 'song of the season'.

▼ *Wildebeest seen on the banks of the Mara river, after which the game reserve Masai Mara is named*

Conservation of Endangered Mammals

We share our planet with a variety of flora and fauna, and all species have an equal right to call it home. Apart from that, they make the world we live in beautiful and interesting. They provide for many of our needs; for example we get wool from sheep and milk from cows. Upon visiting a nature park, one thing we all look for are animals. So, is it not our duty to contribute toward saving the animals?

Ways to Help

- Educate people about the importance of animals.
- Make the world in which animals live a better place for them to inhabit. It could be done by cleaning up human waste from their surroundings—removing plastic and other harmful waste thrown around in parks and beaches.
- Volunteer at a zoo, aquarium, or natural reserve in your area.

▲ Many animals form large herds for migration

Let us look at a few animals from around the world which need our help. We may not have seen them if they live in faraway lands. But every animal in this world counts and if they are not conserved, the vast diversity of animals we see might be lost forever.

▲ The Sahara Conservation Fund is active in protecting the addax

Lost in the Desert

Addax is a desert antelope known to live in harsh environments. These antelopes are active during nights, since in the daytime they dig into the sand and stay under cover to keep away from the hot desert sun. Once found in abundance around Sahara in Africa, they now live in a confined area between Niger and Chad.

Sadly, this animal is in the Critically Endangered Red List of IUCN. A protected population exists in the Yotvata Hai-Bar Nature Reserve in Israel. Soon, Niger will have a vast area reserved to protect the remaining animals that move in the wild.

The dwindling number of the addax is mainly due to hunting. This mammal's meat and leather are useful commodities purchased by the local people. Droughts and a shrinking habitat also contribute to their endangerment.

The Spotted Predator

The Asiatic cheetah has long legs, a spotted coat, and a slender frame. It is one of the fastest runners on land. Once upon a time, these animals abounded the Indian sub-continent, Afghanistan, and Central Asia. However, now they fall under the Critically Endangered list of the IUCN. The animals prefer to live in plains and desert-like areas.

Today, their population is concentrated in a remote region of Iran. This reduced population was caused by the loss of prey and hunting activity. The government of Iran is working with various wildlife agencies to create a programme which might save this animal in one of its last reserves.

▼ There are only about 50 Asiatic cheetahs remaining in Iran

Word Check

Blowhole: The nostril at the top of a whale or dolphin's head

Blubber: It is the fat in a sea mammal's body that keeps it warm.

Browsing: It refers to animals feeding on vegetation that grows on trees like leaves and twigs from trees.

Carapace: It is the hard, upper shell structure of a mammal like a glyptodont or tortoise.

Diurnal: It refers to animals that are active during the day and rest during the night.

Dorsal: It refers to the upper area or back of an animal.

Echolocation: It is the method of using sound waves and echoes to understand where different objects are placed in a path.

Endothermy: The ability to generate heat and regulate the body temperature internally

Ethologist: It refers to a person involved in ethology—the study of animal behaviour focusing on the patterns that they exhibit in their natural environment.

Foetus: It refers to an unborn vertebrate that is still developing.

Hair follicles: It is a part of the skin formed by padding old cells together. Hair grows from hair follicles.

Incubate: It refers to the process by which birds sit on the eggs that they lay to keep them warm before they hatch.

Marsupials: An animal species whose female lacks enough placenta and has a pouch on the abdomen in which she carries the young to feed and nurture it

Monotreme: It is a mammalian order of egg-laying animals like the duck-billed platypus.

Moult: It means to shed old feathers, skin, or fur.

Nocturnal: It refers to animals that are active during the night and rest during the day.

Omnivorous: It refers to an animal that eats both plants and other animals.

Opposable thumb: It means that the thumb can be held opposite to the other fingers on the hand. Hands with opposable thumbs can form fists to hold objects.

Paleontologist: It refers to a person who studies palaeontology—the branch of science that deals with fossils of dead animals and plants.

Pectoral fins: They are the fins present on either sides of mammals such as dolphins. They reside just behind the mammal's head.

Placenta: It refers to an organ that is temporary. Its function is to join the mother to the foetus in a way that the transfer of oxygen, nutrients, and waste becomes easier.

Savannahs: They are open plains in the tropics that are covered with grass and little trees.

Umbilical cord: It exists in animals that have placenta while giving birth. It is a pipe between the placenta and the developing foetus.

Vertebrates: It refers to animals that have backbones or spinal cords covered with bones.

Viviparous: It refers to a group of animals that reproduce by live birth instead of reproducing by laying eggs.